LET'S VISIT CZECHOSLOVAKIA

DISCARD

J
914.37
P

45729

Let's visit
CZECHOSLOVAKIA

JULIAN POPESCU

BURKE

First published April 1970
Second revised edition 1983
© Julian Popescu 1970 and 1983

All rights reserved. No part of this publication may be reproduced, stored in a retrieval system, or transmitted, in any form or by any means, electronic, mechanical, photocopying, recording or otherwise, without the prior permission of Burke Publishing Company Limited.

ACKNOWLEDGEMENTS

The author and publishers are grateful to the following for permission to reproduce copyright photographs in this book:

David Cohen; the Czechoslovak Embassy; Keystone Press Agency Ltd.; Russ Kinne and Bruce Coleman Ltd.; The Mansell Collection; Paul Popper Ltd.; Mrs E. Preston; Roger Randall; the Romanian Embassy; Skyport Fotos; Syndication International; United Press International (U.K.) Ltd.

The cover photograph of the Town Hall Square, Prague, is reproduced by permission of Camera Press Ltd.

CIP data
Popescu, Julian
    Let's visit Czechoslovakia. – 2nd ed.
    1. Czechoslovakia – Social life and customs –
Juvenile literature
    I. Title
    943.7   DB215
    ISBN 0 222 00923 3

Burke Publishing Company Limited
Pegasus House, 116–120 Golden Lane, London EC1Y 0TL, England.
Burke Publishing (Canada) Limited
Toronto, Ontario, Canada.
Burke Publishing Company Inc.
540 Barnum Avenue, Bridgeport, Connecticut 06608, U.S.A.
Filmset in 'Monophoto' Baskerville by Green Gates Studios, Hull, England.
Printed in Singapore by Tien Wah Press (Pte.) Ltd.

Contents

ECHOSLOVAKIA

MILES

0   100

KILOMETRES

0   160

OLAND

R. Morava

Ostrava

HIGH TATRAS

Zilina

Poprad

R. Vah

LOW TATRAS

Levoca

Presov

Kosice

O S L O V A K I A

WHITE CARPATHIANS

Bratislava

R. Danube

U.S.S.R.

HUNGARY

AM

Bullocks like these are a useful form of transport for Slovak farmers

In the Heart of Europe

The map of Europe includes a long and narrow country, shaped like a caterpillar, which lies right in the middle of the continent. This country is Czechoslovakia, a land of ancient towns and castles, of rugged mountains and hills with magnificent scenery; it is also a land with vast forests of prime timber, and with fertile valleys and rolling plains which stretch as far as the eye can see into the distant horizon.

Though small in size, Czechoslovakia has a varied climate with cold winters and hot summers. She is rich in natural resources (such as timber and coal) and the western part of the country is highly industrialized; it has many iron and steel mills and factories which make precision instruments, shoes and cars.

Today Czechoslovakia is a Socialist Republic; she is also a Communist country. With an area of 49,362 square miles (127,878 square kilometres) the country is about the size of England. But, by contrast with England, Czechoslovakia is land-locked and very distant from the sea. In spite of this, Czechoslovakia has exits to three seas: to the Black Sea via the River Danube which is an important international waterway, to the North Sea via the River Elbe and to the Baltic Sea via the River Oder.

Czechoslovakia's central position in Europe and her broad valleys have made her a meeting-place of highways from north, south, east and west. This is why the country is often described as being at the crossroads of Europe.

The Czechoslovaks are a good-humoured people with an artistic temperament. They are also industrious and hard-working. They belong to the Slav family of peoples and are related to the Poles, Russians, Yugoslavs and Bulgarians. The Czechoslovaks feel strongly about their kinship with other Slavs.

The Czechoslovaks themselves consist of two nations, the Czechs and the Slovaks. The Czechs are mostly industrial workers while the Slovaks are peasant farmers. They speak different languages and eat different food. The Czech and Slovak languages are both Slavonic languages (as are Polish and Russian) and many Czech and Slovak words resemble Polish or Russian. More than two-thirds of Czechoslovakia's population of over fifteen million are Czechs. The majority of the rest of the population are Slovaks with the addition of large German, Hungarian, Polish and Ukrainian communities.

Czechoslovakia is a new country which was formed after the First World War (1914–18) when the Austro-Hungarian Empire was defeated and many of its former provinces became national states. In the Middle Ages the greater part of present-day Czechoslovakia was known as the Kingdom of Bohemia.

Slovak farm-workers gathering in the hay. Women often help on the land in Czechoslovakia

The kings of Bohemia were rich and powerful and were related to many of the other kings of Europe. Queen Anne, the wife of the English King Richard II, was the daughter of King Charles of Bohemia. She is buried in Westminster Abbey.

In 1939 (at the beginning of the Second World War), the German army marched into Prague, the Czechoslovak capital. Western Czechoslovakia was turned into a German protectorate while the other half of the country became the new Republic of Slovakia. The Czechs suffered great persecution under the Germans and many of them were killed. Towards the end of the war the country became a battlefield with both Russian and American troops fighting the Germans. The last battles of the Second World War took place in Czechoslovakia, leaving behind ruined cities, damaged bridges and railways, and burnt-out farms. Because of the destruction and damage, food was scarce and expensive and many people went about dressed in rags.

Since then many things have changed. The Czechoslovak people worked hard to repair the war damage. They built new factories and opened new mines; roads were widened and improved and slums cleared away. The peasant farmers were given tractors and other machinery to till the land on large, co-operative farms. After a few years, factories began to turn out the goods to fill the shops while the farms produced enough to make food plentiful again.

The Czechoslovaks use money called crowns or *korunas*. Each crown consists of one hundred hellers, which makes it a decimal currency. One heller is worth nothing but you can buy a small bun for about fifty hellers. No one can take crowns, however small a quantity, out of the country; nor are they allowed to bring any Czechoslovak money in from abroad.

Ever since the Communists came to power in Czechoslovakia in 1948, the country has been ruled by one political party. The Czechoslovak Communist rulers signed a treaty of alliance with the U.S.S.R. which still gives the Russians power to decide the country's home and foreign policy. In 1968, the Russians feared that the Czechoslovak people wanted their country to be free and independent, so they sent their tanks and troops to occupy important Czechoslovak towns and air-fields.

Today Czechoslovakia is a very busy country. The roads carry heavy motor traffic between industrial cities. Farms produce large quantities of vegetables and fruit which are exported all over Europe. Each year many foreign tourists go to Czechoslovakia to visit the ancient cities and castles, to rest at the beautiful spas of Bohemia or to climb the rocky mountains of Slovakia.

Czechoslovakia is an hospitable country whose people want to live the western way of life because throughout their history they have belonged to the western world. Castles, palaces and cathedrals built in the German Gothic and Italian baroque style can be seen in many towns of the country. Some of the castles are old medieval forts such as Karlstejn Castle near Prague and Orava Castle in the north of Slovakia, defended

Karlstejn Castle, near Prague. This mediaeval fort commands the surrounding
countryside

by thick walls and tall towers. Other castles stand high and lonely on rocky summits. They have stout ramparts and narrow windows. What hard work it must have been to carry all the heavy stones up the steep and narrow paths to build them!

In days gone by the powerful lords of these castles lived in rooms hung with expensive tapestries and furnished with carved oak chests and chairs. They dined by torchlight in banqueting-halls, listening to the jokes of jesters and watching the embers glow in the huge fireplaces. Today many of these splendid castles are in ruins, their blackened walls covered by moss and weeds. But some of them have been restored and rebuilt and turned into museums and open-air theatres for people to visit and enjoy. Large parking places for cars have been built below the ancient castles and cable cars make it easy to reach the castle gates.

Now let us visit friendly Czechoslovakia and learn more about the character of her land and people.

13

Geography and Climate

Czechoslovakia has long land frontiers which run mostly along high mountains and hills. She has six neighbours. To the north is Poland with whom she has the longest common frontier— nearly nine hundred miles (1,390 kilometres). East Germany is to the north-east while West Germany is to the south-west. In the south, Czechoslovakia borders Austria and Hungary. Part of the frontier with Hungary runs along the middle of the River Danube. Here Czechoslovakia and Hungary work together to harness the waters of the Danube for the production of hydro-electric power and to improve the waterway on which passenger steamers and huge barges laden with goods travel for long distances.

The U.S.S.R. is Czechoslovakia's mighty and feared neighbour to the east. The border between the two countries is less than sixty miles long (98 kilometres). This border was fixed by the Russians at the end of the Second World War when the eastern tip of Czechoslovakia, known as Subcarpathian Ruthenia, was absorbed into the U.S.S.R. An important highway and a railway now cross the border into the U.S.S.R. The road makes for easy communication between the two countries. This was a great advantage to Russia when her tanks and troops swiftly invaded Czechoslovakia in the summer of 1968.

Eastern Czechoslovakia, the land between Hungary and Poland, is called Slovakia. The northern half of this land is mountainous and poor farming land. But in the summer shepherds bring their flocks of sheep and goats to graze the high alpine meadows.

Southern Slovakia is a vast rolling plain which is fertile because rich mud is deposited there by torrents and rivers from the mountains. Many thousands of years ago the Miocene Sea covered the plain, reaching to the foot of the mountains; but, because of earth movements, the level of the sea gradually fell and it dried up, leaving only the plain behind.

The mountains of Slovakia are called the Carpathians; they are a southern continuation of the Alps. They stretch in an arc across western and northern Slovakia and then cross the border into the U.S.S.R. In the west the mountains are called the White Carpathians and the hard granite rocks have a bright appearance because they contain grains of quartz and mica. The lower slopes of the mountains are covered with forest plantations of evergreen trees—fir and spruce. The

A startled chamois beneath a granite outcrop in the Carpathians

Mountain walking, a popular sport in the High Tatras

region also has a few gold- and silver-mines in the valleys which are still being worked.

In the north there are two mountain ranges—the High Tatras and the Low Tatras—famous for their beautiful scenery. The highest peaks of the Carpathians are located in the High Tatras only a short distance from the Polish border. Mount Gerlach (8,735 feet/2,663 metres) is the highest, and nearby Mount Lomnica is 8,641 feet (2,634 metres) high.

These mountains are composed of limestone and crystalline rocks. They are bare and rocky with narrow, pointed ridges cut by ice in the distant past. There are many lakes of clear blue water in the deep hollows similar to those known in Scotland as corries. The corries have a semi-circular shape and have been worn away by glaciers. Geologists describe this type of country as glaciated.

In the regions where there are limestone rocks, long caves are hidden deep underground. They are made by the action of water which wears away the rock. These caves are often

16

connected with each other. On their roofs they have stony icicles called stalactites. A huge glacier lies buried in one of these caves; it has been preserved intact from the Ice Age.

Vegetation is poor on the Tatra Mountains and is not encouraged by the climate. The high foot-hills are covered with snow until late in May. Only mosses, brambles, brushwood and stunted birch trees grow there, though lower down there are valuable forests of spruce, fir and pine trees. Ferns and brightly-coloured wild flowers grow in clearings where the trees have been cut.

The golden eagle with its feathered legs and hooked beak can be seen here, circling the valleys in search of wild game. These birds of prey often nest on a craggy ledge among the rocks. Wild animals, such as the chamois (which can stand with all four legs on a sharp peak of rock) and the moufflon

The golden eagle, whose vicious beak helps to kill its prey

A polecat. Its sharp
claws are useful
for tree-climbing

or wild sheep, live there. A few brown bears live in the forests.
Squirrels and polecats climb the trees, while stags roam the
valleys. Wolves are found there too; in summer, they shelter
in remote valleys; in winter, they come down to attack flocks
of sheep and goats on the farms. The whole of the Tatra
Mountain area has been declared by law a nature reserve.
This means that no wild animals can be hunted or killed for
sport there.

The plain of southern Slovakia is part of the Danube Valley.
Although the average yearly rainfall is low, the land near the
Danube has poor drainage and includes vast marshes broken
only by islands of willow trees, rushes and reeds. Wild duck,

A mountain wolf. In winter,
wolves sometimes attack flocks
of sheep and goats in Czechoslovakia

geese and storks live on these islands, and cormorants diving for fish and swimming under water, are a familiar sight.

Fishermen and hunters of wildfowl use long, flat-bottomed boats to cross the marshes. An unusual inhabitant of the area is the giant catfish, which sometimes grows to an enormous size and weight, and lives in muddy stretches of the Danube near by. It has no scales but it does have razor-sharp teeth and it often kills and eats wildfowl. It has been known to attack children swimming in the river.

Some of the Danube marshes have been enclosed with dykes of stone and earth and drained for farming. Good crops of melons, cucumbers and other vegetables are grown there.

Western and central Czechoslovakia, also known as the Czech lands, consist of three regions called Bohemia, Moravia and Silesia.

Bohemia lies in the west of the country and is shaped like a diamond. Its centre is a plateau of gently sloping hills and broad valleys. The River Vltava, on which there are several dams, reservoirs and hydro-electric power-stations, runs northwards through the middle of the plateau.

These flat-bottomed boats are used where the water is shallow

Bohemia is bordered on all sides by mountains which are cut by deep gorges. To the north are the Ore Mountains and the Giant Mountains which, in spite of their name, are not very high. These mountains are very ancient and their summits have been worn away by wind and rain. Their highest peaks are Mount Arber which rises to 4,780 feet (1,457 metres) and Mount Rachell which is 4,764 feet (1,452 metres) high.

It can be very cold in the Bohemian mountains in winter. Their slopes are covered with snow until early spring and are popular with skiers. But when the hot dry wind (known as the *Föhn*) blows from the south, a sudden thaw sets in and torrents of water pour down the mountain-sides.

Because of the *Föhn* wind and prevailing westerly winds the climate of Bohemia is milder than that of the rest of Czechoslovakia. The average winter temperature is 31° Fahrenheit ($-0.5°$ Centigrade) while the average temperature in summer is 67° Fahrenheit (19° Centigrade).

Large forests of spruce and Scots fir used to cover Bohemia but now many of the trees have been cut for timber and the land has been taken over for farming. Where the land has been left untouched, bushes and weeds provide good hiding-places for wild game. Hares, pheasants and wild boar live there, while stags and herds of deer roam the open country.

The mountains of Bohemia are rich in coal, iron ore, lead, copper and other minerals and there are many factories built near the mines. There are also quarries in the hills which produce quartz from which the fine Bohemian glass is made.

Skiers approaching a high peak in the Giant Mountains

In addition, oil and methane gas are extracted in the south.

The valleys are intensively cultivated. Farmers rear dairy cattle and pigs and grow rye, barley and hops which are used for flavouring lager and other beers.

Moravia and Silesia form central Czechoslovakia. Moravia takes its name from the River Morava, a major tributary of the Danube, which flows from the north through the middle of the region.

The Moravian lowlands lie between the highlands of Bohemia and the Carpathian Mountains. The broad Morava valley is a natural route between the North European Plain and the Danube Valley. In fact, it was such an important route between north and south in the Middle Ages that many castles were built along it to guard river crossings and important market towns.

Much of the land in the Morava valley consists of chestnut-coloured or black earth. Farmers grow good crops of wheat, barley and potatoes there. They also have plantations of flax and hemp which are used as raw materials for the textile industry. Cattle graze in enclosed fields, while vines are cultivated on the sunny slopes of hills.

21

Recently, oil and methane gas deposits have been found in the Moravian uplands in the south and, when extracted, they are carried by pipeline to the industrial towns.

Silesia lies near the Polish border, in the upper basin of the River Oder, which rises in the Carpathian Mountains and then meanders northwards into Poland. Silesia is also called the Black Country, because of its many factories and the smoke pouring from their tall chimneys. It is one of the great industrial centres of Europe. The area has large deposits of brown coal (lignite) and coal suitable for coking, as well as zinc and rock-salt mines. The chemical coking plants and iron- and steel-mills built near the collieries now use more coke than is produced locally. For this reason, extra coke is imported from the rich coalfield in Polish Silesia across the border.

Western Silesia is hilly and mountainous with dense forests and holiday resorts. The forests are full of wildlife. Deer, squirrels and lynxes live there. The cat-like lynx can easily be recognized by its tufted ear tips, short tail and spotted coat. It is a fierce and cruel animal which kills for pleasure and not just for food. For this reason lynxes are not protected by game laws and can be shot on sight.

The attractive-looking lynx is a killer in disguise and there is no law to prevent its being shot

The eastern part of Silesia is fertile lowland with big farms growing vegetables for sale in the industrial towns.

Early History and the Middle Ages

Thousands of years ago the Czechs and Slovaks lived on the grassy plains of Central Asia and Russia. They wandered from place to place, living in tents, tilling the ground and rearing cattle and horses. They were not a warlike people but were content with their life and at peace with their neighbours.

Then barbarians from Mongolia and the Central Asian lands began to cross the plains into Europe to plunder the rich settlements there. One tribe of barbarians, called the Avars, conquered the Czechs and Slovaks in the early centuries after the birth of Christ. The Avars drove the Czechs and Slovaks westwards, often using them as slave workers. As a result, towards the end of the fifth century and throughout the sixth century, the Czechs and Slovaks settled in the valleys and forest clearing of their present country. In about A.D. 620 their chieftain, whose name was Samo, led his people in an uprising. They defeated the Avars in battle and gained their freedom.

The Czechs and Slovaks established permanent settlements in their new lands. They built wooden or stone houses which they decorated with carvings of leaves, flowers and animals. The houses had no chimneys except for a square hole in the roof above the hearth. When a fire was lit in the hearth, the

23

rooms were heavy with smoke. To defend the settlements, they surrounded them with deep ditches and with steep banks topped by sharp stakes to keep out marauders.

The new settlers were heathen. They worshipped their gods in small temples and killed goats, horses and cows as sacrifices. Then the men, women and children feasted on the meat of the dead animals.

In the eighth century A.D. the Christian Emperor Michael of Byzantium heard about the heathen Czechs and Slovaks and sent two missionary brothers from Thessalonika in Greece to preach the Christian faith to them. These two brothers were Constantine and Methodius; they brought the Christian faith to all the Slav peoples and taught them how to read and write, using the Cyrillic alphabet which they developed from the Greek alphabet. Later, the Czechs and Slovaks came under the influence of Roman Catholic missionaries and so joined the Catholic faith.

Later still, the Slovaks who lived on the northern banks of the Danube were conquered by the Hungarians and were ruled by them for nearly one thousand years until they became independent again at the end of the First World War (1918). Meanwhile, the Czechs founded the Kingdom of Bohemia which became an important European state in the Middle Ages.

One of the earliest kings of Bohemia became known all over western Europe as a royal saint. He was Good King Wenceslas. In many ways he resembled King Edward the Martyr of

24

Wenceslas Square Prague, named after "Good King Wenceslas". Trams are used for public transport in Prague, and traffic congestion is a problem

England. King Wenceslas ruled for only a few years because he was murdered when he was still young, in A.D. 929, by his brother—Boleslav the Cruel. People all over the world still remember King Wenceslas in the popular Christmas carol.

Another interesting king of Bohemia was King John, who ruled the country from 1310 to 1346. He was a brave king who, though blind, fought many battles in knight's armour. When he heard that King Edward III of England had invaded France he went to the help of his French cousin King Philip. The two kings met Edward III in battle at Crécy in 1346. King John fought with great courage but was killed. King Edward honoured the dead king by bringing his body into his own tent. The Black Prince, who was present, was deeply impressed by the dead king's crest and motto: three ostrich feathers and the words *Ich Dien*, "I serve". He adopted this crest and motto which have been ever since the crest and

25

St Vitus
Cathedral was
founded in
A.D. 930 by
King Wenceslas
and rebuilt by
Charles IV in
the Gothic
style. It stands
in the centre
of the Royal
Palace in
Prague

motto of the Princes of Wales. Thus was established the first direct link between the kingdoms of England and Bohemia.

King John was followed on the throne by King Charles IV who became famous because he built a castle and a great Benedictine monastery near Prague. In the city itself he built the Cathedral of St Vitus and the famous Charles Bridge. King Charles, who was a great scholar, also founded the University of Prague in 1348. This university soon became famous and rivalled the universities of Oxford and Paris; for many years students from all parts of Europe came to study there.

26

In the late fourteenth century a fiery preacher called Jan Huss, one of the early leaders of the Protestant movement, lived in the Kingdom of Bohemia. Like the English reformer John Wycliffe, he taught the people to find Christian truth by reading the Bible. The Roman Catholic Church was angered by the teachings of Jan Huss and brought him to trial as a heretic. He was found guilty and burnt at the stake in 1415. Soon all his followers were persecuted as heretics and many Bohemians fled their country and found refuge in Germany and France. Being poor, the Bohemians lived like gypsies. That is why nowadays we often call people who live like gypsies or more colourfully than ourselves "Bohemian".

In the early seventeenth century the Kingdom of Bohemia was conquered by the Austrians. Later, it became a province of the Austro-Hungarian Empire. But, though they remained a subjected people for three centuries, the Czechs never lost their national pride; and they longed to be free and independent again.

The memorial in Prague which commemorates Jan Huss, the Protestant reformer

Recent History and Independence

The most powerful rulers of the Austrian Empire were the Hapsburgs who came to the throne of Austria in the thirteenth century. Their empire grew steadily until it stretched from the Adriatic Sea to the Carpathian Mountains and included the whole of present-day Czechoslovakia.

The Czechs and Slovaks suffered severely under the rule of the Austrians who governed their lands with the help of landowners and nobles. Anyone who criticized the government was thrown into gaol. The peasants' livelihood was linked to the land; they had no freedom and they lived in poverty. Often there were riots in the villages and these were cruelly put down by mounted police armed with swords. Matters grew worse when, in the middle of the nineteenth century, the Emperor of Austria also became King of Hungary; and the Austrian Empire became the Austro-Hungarian Empire. Taxes on the Czechs, Slovaks and other subject peoples were increased to pay for the running of the new empire. When the First World War broke out, Austro-Hungary joined in the war on the side of the Germans. Most of the fighting was done on the eastern front against the Russians and many Czech and Slovak soldiers deserted rather than fight for their foreign masters.

The end of the First World War also meant the end of the Austro-Hungarian Empire. In 1919, Czechoslovakia was given her independence at the Treaty of Versailles and Thomas Masaryk became the first President of the new Republic.

Under his rule the country flourished and the people were happy.

Misfortune came again to Czechoslovakia in 1938 when Adolf Hitler claimed a part of the country for Germany. The British Prime Minister, Neville Chamberlain, went to Munich to have talks with Hitler about Czechoslovakia. But, a year later, Hitler's troops marched into Prague and the Czech lands were turned into a German protectorate. During the Second World War (1939–1945) the Czechs set up secret organizations to resist the Germans. But the Germans behaved cruelly towards the population. People in Czechoslovakia still recall with horror how the Germans destroyed the village of Lidice and killed all its inhabitants as a reprisal for the shooting of the merciless German Governor of Prague.

After the end of the Second World War, with the world still

A German tank is saluted by inhabitants of a town in Western Czechoslovakia during the German invasion of 1939

Harvesting sugar beet on a farm near the town of Cheb, Bohemia

in turmoil, the Communists saw their chance in Czecho-slovakia. In 1948 they took over the government and banned all other political parties. They also prevented newspapers and publishers printing what they liked as they had before.

The Czechoslovak government decided to base the running of the country on the socialist system of production. Banks, factories, mines, hotels and shops were all nationalized—being taken over by the State. Landowners were forced to give away their estates, which were turned into co-operative farms. Even forests and vineyards became public property. Plans were made for developing the country with the help of the U.S.S.R.

In 1948 Czechoslovakia joined the "Cominform" which is an alliance of Communist countries. A year later she joined the "Comecon" or Common Market of the Communist countries. Then, in 1954, Czechoslovakia joined the Warsaw Pact which is a military alliance of Communist countries similar to the western defence system called the North Atlantic Treaty Organization.

Czechoslovakia was a founder member of the United Nations Organization. As a Communist country, her representatives at the United Nations General Assembly have always voted in favour of the resolutions put forward by the U.S.S.R. and other Communist countries. So Czechoslovakia has been regarded by the western countries as a satellite of the U.S.S.R.

When the Communist government of Czechoslovakia came to power, it decided to keep the country's old coat-of-arms except for the old crown and cross and a few other minor changes. The new coat-of-arms is a white lion with two tails, standing on his rear legs against the background of a red shield. Above the lion's head there is a small star. The lion carries a small shield which represents the Slovak coat-of-arms consisting of three hills and a torch above. The country's flag has remained unchanged and is divided into two bands, one white and one red, with a blue triangle placed on the left side over the two bands.

The New Czechs and Slovaks

The Czechs and Slovaks settled in the middle of Europe in the early Dark Ages. Centuries later they came under different rulers. The Slovaks were conquered by the Hungarians who came from the plains of the south; and, later still, the Czechs were forced to join the Austrian Empire.

Then, after independence and union in the twentieth century, the Czech lands and Slovakia became known as the Czechoslovak Republic. So the new Czechs and Slovaks have lived in their present country for less than a century. But even during this period there have been great changes in Czechoslovakia's borders and government. When the Communists came to power in 1948 they called the country the Czechoslovak People's Democratic Republic. In 1960 it became known as the Czechoslovak Socialist Republic. And, on January 1st, 1969, Czechoslovakia became a federal state, or union of states, like the United States of America. The new federal state consists of two republics: the Czech Socialist Republic and the Slovak Socialist Republic. The Czechs and

There have been constant changes in Czecho-slovakia's borders. These peasants are natives of Ruthenia, once Czechoslovak, now Russian

Slovaks have equal rights and they are equally represented in the federal government and parliament.

The Czech Socialist Republic forms the western part of the country. Most of its inhabitants are Czechs but some of them are descendants of German settlers. The area of the Republic is 30,442 square miles (78,866 square kilometres). The capital, Prague, is situated on the banks of the River Vltava. It is the most important industrial town in the whole of Czechoslovakia. Its population is over one million.

East of the Czech lands and the Carpathian Mountains is the Slovak Socialist Republic. This is the smaller of the two republics; it has an area of 18,920 square miles (49,012 square kilometres). Its inhabitants, who are of Slovak and Hungarian descent, are great farmers. The capital, Bratislava, is a busy port on the Danube and has a population of nearly three hundred thousand.

The law states that the Czechoslovak Federal Assembly, or parliament, which meets in Prague is the supreme authority in the state. The Federal Assembly has two chambers: the House of the People and the House of the Nations. Both Houses are elected for four years. The House of the People has two hundred members of which 138 are Czechs and sixty-two Slovaks. The House of Nations has one hundred and fifty members; half of them are Czechs and the others are Slovaks. Unlike the British parliament and those modelled on it, the Czechoslovak House of the People has no "Opposition" members.

Bratislava, seat of the Slovak National Council

The Head of State is called the President and he is elected for five years by the Federal Assembly. The President has his offices and residence in Prague Castle. The federal government in Prague is elected for a period of four years.

The Czech lands and Slovakia have their own elected parliaments, known as National Councils. The Czech National Council has two hundred members while the Slovak National Council has one hundred and fifty members. These Councils pass laws dealing with education and with the health and welfare services. The administration of the Czech lands and Slovakia is carried out by a separate government with its own Prime Minister.

Both the Czech lands and Slovakia are divided into a

34

number of regions for the purpose of local government. In each region there is a national committee which deals with local problems, such as the building of schools or houses, refuse collection and the provision of drinking water.

The new Czechs and Slovaks are proud of their country and are intensely patriotic. They work hard at their jobs and do much voluntary service in the federal and local governments.

Though they belong to a small country, many Czechoslovaks have become world-famous. Emil Zatopek, the champion long-distance runner, and the gymnast Vera Caslavska who won three gold medals at the Mexico Olympic Games are both Czechs. And Franz Kafka, one of the modern world's great writers, was born in Prague. Thomas Masaryk (who was Czechoslovakia's first President) and his son Jan Masaryk are both considered to have been among Europe's great statesmen.

Entrance to Prague Castle, home of the President of Czechoslovakia

In another, very different walk of life was Vladimir Remek who won fame as a cosmonaut in 1978 when he went in a spaceship round the Earth with his Russian fellow-cosmonaut Aleksey Gubarev.

Bren Guns and Pilsen Beer

Industry and mining have a long tradition in Czechoslovakia. In the Middle Ages the cities of Bohemia and Moravia were famous for their skilled craftsmen who were organized in guilds and who made fine jewels, glassware and pottery. Gold and silver were mined and used for minting coins in the earliest times, but it was only at the beginning of the nineteenth century that industry based on coal and iron began to be developed on a large scale in the Czech lands, which soon became the industrial heart of the Austro-Hungarian Empire.

At the beginning of the twentieth century, the people of Czechoslovakia manufactured a great variety of products. They made railway-engines and wagons, rifles and guns, textiles, furniture and musical instruments, shoes and carpets, beer and medicines, paper, sugar and sweets. Since independence, in 1918, Czechoslovakia has developed into an important industrial nation and her manufactured goods are exported all over the world.

Today Czechoslovakia is a Communist country. Banks and mines were nationalized in 1946. Then all factories, transport and shops became State property. Private ownership is not allowed. Individuals cannot own a factory or open a shop. All production and distribution is planned by the government with the aim of developing engineering, the manufacture of chemicals and other branches of industry for the export trade. When production is planned in advance for a five-year period it is called a Five-Year Plan. There have been several such plans since 1948.

Czechoslovak industry is based on coal which is mined from rich deposits in central and northern Bohemia and in Silesia. Czechoslovakia occupies seventh position in the world in the production of coal. Some of the collieries have now been abandoned because they have been worked too long. Their place has been taken by new pits which are easier to work because they have modern cutting machinery and conveyor-belts.

Iron ore, copper and zinc, gold and silver, lead, uranium, antimony and bauxite have all been found in the uplands of

A delicatessen shop in Prague. All shops and factories are now owned by the State

Bohemia. In some places engineers have opened the rocky sides of the hills by blasting. In other places they have bored deep tunnels. After this, the miners break up the ore with pneumatic drills. Automatic shovels lift the ore into railway trucks which go to crushing- and cleaning-plants located near the mines.

Among other useful minerals mined in Czechoslovakia are rock salt, and magnesite which is found in large quantities in Silesia. Graphite, which is used for making pencils, is mined in western Slovakia while kaolin, for ceramics, is extracted near Pilsen. Limestone is also quarried for cement-making in Bohemia, Moravia and Slovakia. Today Czechoslovakia occupies thirteenth place in the world for the production of cement.

Czechoslovakia's mineral wealth and skilled labour have made her into an important engineering country. Engineering factories and plants are concentrated in the industrial belt of western and northern Bohemia, around Prague, Brno and Bratislava. Machines of every kind are made: turbines, boilers, tractors, generators, pumps and precision instruments, such as microscopes.

When it comes to working with metal, Czechoslovak workers have the skill to make almost anything, including deadly weapons of war. Brno is the centre of the Czechoslovak armaments industry. Tanks and armoured cars and weapons of all descriptions are made there for use by the Czechoslovak armed forces. But many arms and crates of ammunition are also exported. The manufacture of weapons, sad to say, brings in a lot of money. It was in Brno that the automatic "Bren" gun was invented before the Second World War. This famous gun was then made in Britain under licence at Enfield. (The Moravian city of Brno and the English town of Enfield together gave their names to the Bren gun.)

Another important industry in Czechoslovakia is the brewing of beer and lager. The country is the world's sixth largest producer of beer. Most of the beer is brewed from barley and hops in the cities of Bohemia and Moravia. The bottles of lager brewed at Pilsen are known all over the world as "Pilsner". Many breweries and bottling plants are located in Prague and at Ceske Budejovice near the Austrian border in southern Bohemia.

Pilsner beer is a popular drink in Czechoslovakia

The brewing of beer in Bohemia goes back to the Middle Ages. At that time, city guilds vied with each other to obtain the royal privilege to brew. Oak barrels of beer were then dispatched by pack-horse or brewer's dray to Vienna and other Austrian towns. The beer trade made the brewers and merchants of Bohemia wealthy.

Recently the Czechoslovaks have realized that the fast-flowing rivers of their country are an important source of power. The demand for electricity for homes, factories and mines continues to grow. Several major rivers, such as the Vltava in Bohemia and the Vah in Slovakia, have been changed beyond all recognition. High concrete dams now span these rivers. Behind the dams the waters have gathered, drowning islands, submerging trees and abandoned houses, and forming vast artificial lakes in former valleys. In this way the rivers are made to work to produce hydro-electric power, while the new lakes have become the playground of yachtsmen and water-skiers.

Ordinary power-stations have been built near the coalfields of the north, using cheap coal as fuel for the production of electricity. More and more pylons made of reinforced concrete and gleaming steel stand like giant masts in valleys and on hill-tops, linked by high-tension wires, carrying electric power to cities and villages.

Czechoslovak engineers continue to search for new sources of power. Already they have drawn up plans, in co-operation with Hungarian engineers, to build a dam across the Danube, and a power-station. The dam will have a huge lock to enable ships and barges to pass through it. The electricity produced by the new station will be shared equally by the two countries.

Now, too, peaceful fields in the plains north of Bratislava have been churned up by tip-lorries and bulldozers. The whole place is alive with the hum of engines and clang of steel girders. Here work has been started on building the first nuclear power-station in Czechoslovakia. Plans are also being made for building nuclear power-stations in other parts of the country.

Czechoslovak prospectors and geologists have found oil and natural gas in southern Moravia. The quantities of oil and gas produced by the wells are not large but they help to cut the import bill. Most of the crude oil Czechoslovakia uses is imported from Russia through a long pipeline which, with its powerful pumping-stations, stretches for a vast distance across the Great Russian Plain to the oilfield near the Caspian Sea. Russians proudly call this pipeline the Friendship Pipeline.

The plentiful supplies of coal in the country and the oil imported from Russia are used as raw materials by the Czecho-slovak chemical industry which produces synthetic fibres, plastic materials, fertilizers, gunpowder, paints and a great variety of drugs and medicines. Many chemical plants are located in Prague, Brno, Ostrava and Bratislava.

Czech craftsmen are famous for the cut glass and porcelain they make. Fine glass tumblers, chandeliers and Christmas tree ornaments are made in small workshops near Prague and

This Czecho-slovak glass is exported to many countries of the world

Karlovy Vary. From there they are exported to many countries of the world.

Czechoslovakia's most modern industry is the making of cars, scooters and motor bicycles. The best-known car models are *Skoda* and *Tatra*, which can be seen on all the country's roads. Both the *Skoda* and the *Tatra* are also exported abroad in large numbers to earn much-needed foreign currency.

Forests and Lumbering

Czechoslovakia is a land of great forests. About one-third of the country is forest land. The great Bohemian Forest stretches across the hills of southern Bohemia and over the border into Austria. But many of the thickest forests in the country are on

42

Coniferous trees in the Tatras. Their wood has many uses

the slopes of the Carpathian Mountains in Slovakia. Some of these forests are called virgin forests because they have never been exploited by man. Coniferous trees such as larch, fir and pine grow in the Carpathians, while the Siberian cedar flourishes in the Tatra range. The trees are straight and tall and very useful for lumber. The pine trees are also tapped for their milky and strong-smelling sap called resin. Deep cuts are made in the bark of the pines and the resin trickles into small cups placed under them. Resin is a valuable raw material used in making medicines, glues and varnishes.

The soft wood of coniferous trees is used for making furniture, skis and matches and in house-building. Czech craftsmen are famed for the church organs and other musical instruments they make from soft wood. No wood is ever wasted; any left over, including small logs and odd-shaped pieces, is cut into chips, then ground into sawdust to be made into pulp. The pulp is used to make paper, cardboard, artificial silk, wood alcohol and plastic materials.

In the hilly parts of the country and in the valleys there are forests of oak, beech, birch, maple and ash. Beech and oak wood are used to make vats, barrels and kegs for Czechoslovakia's important beer industry. These hard woods are also used for making pit-props and railway-sleepers. They also serve as fuel for homes and factories in many parts of the country.

Czechoslovakia has other trees too. In the far south of Slovakia where the summers are hot and dry, there are forests of acacia trees. The sweet-smelling yellow flowers of the acacia produce much nectar which is collected by the honey bee. And in one sheltered valley in western Slovakia there is a forest of edible chestnut trees, some of which are reputed to be four hundred years old!

When winter comes the trees rest, no sap rises and the wood is dry. Then Czech and Slovak lumbermen come to the hills and mountains and prepare to cut the trees. They build camps in the forest clearings. Each camp consists of a cookhouse, toilets and log cabins with bunks to sleep in. The lumberjacks bring provisions and install electricity. Then the camp super-intendent and his foremen mark the trees to be felled with white rings. They choose trees which are straight and tall. They leave the small trees and saplings, so that the forest is not

Logs piled up at the forest camp to await collection. Cows are sometimes harnessed to lumber carts to move them short distances

laid bare and the land exposed to soil erosion in the spring when the snow melts and the heavy rains come.

Next the lumbermen put on steel helmets and start their work with axes and mechanical saws. Each day they fell a large number of trees which are then stripped of their branches and sawn into logs of various lengths. The logs are moved away on makeshift sledges pulled by tractors or even by cows which are not in milk. Some of the bigger logs are rolled down the mountain side or dragged by a winch along a trench dug in the snow.

In the past, logs used to be transported for long distances down streams and rivers. Today this is no longer possible because many of the rivers in Czechoslovakia have been dammed for irrigation and to produce hydro-electric power. So the logs are now carried in lorries or railway-trucks or even by helicopter straight to the sawmills where they are cut into planks

45

and beams. There are many sawmills in Czechoslovakia which employ hundreds of people and look like huge factories. The mills work all the year round supplying timber merchants, furniture factories and carpenters' shops with the wood they need. Large quantities of timber are also exported to countries which have few forests of their own, such as Hungary across the border in the south.

During the dry summer months, when the brambles, bushes and tall grasses in the forests of Czechoslovakia are dry, there is a great danger of fire. The forest rangers tell tourists not to light camp-fires. They also build tall watch-towers of logs from which they can look out for signs of smoke. Some of the watch-towers have a roof over them and bunks in which the forest rangers can sleep at night. Today, forest rangers are equipped with walkie-talkie radios and when they spot a fire they raise the alarm by informing the nearest forestry station or airfield. Fire-fighting planes then take off and spray the fire with chemicals before it has had a chance to spread. In this way many valuable trees and much wild life are saved from destruction every year.

The forest rangers spend much of their time making fire-breaks in the forests. Firebreaks are strips of land kept clear of trees and bushes. Sometimes tractors and ploughs are used to clear them. The firebreaks prevent the sparks and flames of a forest fire from spreading to other parts of the forest.

Co-operative Farming

Before 1948, farms in Czechoslovakia were privately owned. Some of the farms were small plots of land, no bigger than a large garden, which yielded enough food for a family to live on. Other farms were large estates covering vast areas and including much forest land. They belonged to rich land-owners who usually let their lands to tenant farmers to cultivate and keep in good order. When the crops were harvested the tenant farmers brought half the produce to the landowners. But in 1948 the Czechoslovak government nationalized all land and forests (with the exception of small plots and difficult land on hills) and set up co-operative farms. The government made loans to the new farms to buy machinery, fertilizers and livestock. Many farmers were given special training and taught modern methods of farming. In this way better crops were produced and the number of cattle, sheep and pigs increased.

Czechoslovak co-operative farms produce most of the food for the country's population. Not enough wheat for bread is grown, though, so wheat has to be imported from large wheat-

Haymaking with a special type of scythe which is common on Czechoslovak farms

producing countries, such as Hungary or the U.S.S.R. There is not enough meat either, so tinned and fresh meat are imported from abroad. But Czechoslovak farms do produce large quantities of sugar-beet for sending to the sugar mills. Hops and high-quality barley are grown in western Bohemia for turning into malt, which is used to make beer. And both sugar and beer are important foodstuffs exported by Czechoslovakia.

Czechoslovakia also produces large quantities of maize, oats, rye, flax and potatoes. Oats and rye grow well on the hills of Bohemia and Moravia, while flax and potatoes are grown in the valleys because these plants need very fertile land. Large plantations of maize are found in southern Moravia and in the plains of Slovakia.

The hills of western Slovakia have vineyards planted on them in terraces. According to old folk tales, the vines were first planted by a Roman Emperor called Probus to produce wine for his soldiers. Today, the vineyards grow grapes for eating and for use in making high-quality wine for local consumption.

One of Czechoslovakia's most popular crops is the poppy. Both large plantations and small strips of white poppies, shaking their heads in the light breeze, can be seen in all parts of the country, in the plains as well as the hills. When the poppy heads turn brown they are ripe and dry. They are then picked by hand and the black seed is shaken out and stored in boxes. It is used to flavour and decorate cakes and bread.

Picking apples. Fruit of all kinds ripens well in Czechoslovakia's warm summers

Fruit grows well in Czechoslovakia because of the moist springs and hot summers. The valleys of Moravia and Slovakia have rich apple, plum and pear orchards. Soft fruit, such as strawberries, red and black currants are grown by farms in central Bohemia. Most of the fruit is sent to jam factories. Over-ripe fruit is stored in vats to ferment and then to be distilled into brandy. Czechoslovakia is famous for her pear and plum brandies and for bitter liqueurs flavoured with herbs.

More unusual crops are the many medicinal herbs which are picked by farmers in Czechoslovakia. Camomile (a creeping plant with white flowers), lime-tree flowers, mint, parsley roots, the stalks of cherries and even nettle leaves are made into herbal mixtures. The herbs are sent to factories where they are dried, sterilized and packed. Packets of herbs can be

49

bought at any chemist's in the country, and are exported abroad.

Now let us visit a co-operative farm in southern Moravia, not far from the main road leading to the city of Brno. All the fields around are as flat as a pancake. A narrow dirt-track, with potholes in it and deep ruts made by tractor wheels, winds its way from the main road to the co-operative farm entrance which has big wrought-iron gates. The farm buildings are in a compound surrounded by a high fence made of concrete pillars and wire netting painted green.

The main farm building is on the left. The manager's office, canteen and sleeping-quarters are there. On the right we see row upon row of long, white-washed buildings. Cows, horses and pigs are kept there. At the back of the compound there is a tall silo for storing grain and a huge hangar where tractors, harrows, combines and other farming machinery are kept. Next to the hangar there is a huge heap of rotting manure round about which white Leghorn hens and cocks scratch for worms.

The farm manager is a busy man. His farm has dairy cows, bullocks and pigs for fattening. Wheat, barley, fodder and some maize are grown in the fields. But his most important crop is sugar-beet which is worth a lot of money. The tops of the sugar-beet and the pulp which is returned from the sugar mill are used as cattle feed.

The farm manager decides which crops are to be planted

Fruit trees producing an excellent crop in a Bohemian orchard

and what work is to be done by the members of the co-operative whose plots of land were joined together many years ago to form the present farm. Each year the members hold a general meeting at which they vote on the report and accounts of the farm. The money earned by the farm (for wheat, sugar-beet and other crops as well as livestock) is divided up. About one-third of it goes into building new sheds, and buying machinery and seeds. The rest is shared out among the members in proportion to the work they have been doing. At this meeting the manager and his committee for the coming year are elected. If the old manager is popular and successful he is re-elected. If the members of the co-operative farm are dissatisfied with him, they elect a new manager.

Most of the produce of the co-operative farm is sold to State wholesale firms. It is sold at prices fixed by the Ministry of Agriculture which plans the quantity of crops to be grown in

This sugar-beet combine harvester speeds up work on a State farm. It cuts off the leaves, cleans the beets and gathers them into a separate compartment

the whole country for the next year. The Ministry gives co-operative farms production targets to fulfil and it helps them with loans to buy new machinery and fertilizers. If the year is good, the farms usually reach their targets, but if there is a drought or flood the farms fail to deliver the produce expected of them.

Apart from small quantities of vegetables and fruit from private plots (which are sold at stalls in markets), all farm produce in Czechoslovakia is sold in shops owned by the State. The prices of foodstuffs are fixed in advance and do not vary from day to day or season to season. This means that food is sometimes too plentiful in the shops so that it goes to waste and sometimes very scarce or not available at all. It is not unusual for a whole town to be without meat on certains days of the week. For this reason, Czechoslovak housewives get up early in the morning and queue outside butchers' and grocers' shops to buy the food they need for their families.

Transport and Trade

The first railway in Czechoslovakia was built, in Bohemia, by the Austrians in 1825. This railway was not very long; it led to Linz in Austria. The train of wagons was not drawn by a steam-engine but by teams of strong dray horses. The first steam-engine to pull a train out of Prague was seen off in 1845 by an amazed crowd which had assembled at the railway station.

Since then railways have been built in many parts of the country. Today the total length of track is 7,920 miles (13,200 kilometres). Powerful diesel-engines have replaced steam-engines on most lines; with the growth of the electric power industry, over 720 miles (1,200 kilometres) of railway have been electrified. Now the Czechoslovak railway company is owned by the State.

Motor-cars, buses and lorries are the most important means of travel and transport in Czechoslovakia today. There are over half a million motor vehicles in the country. You can travel everywhere by car, even in remote mountain districts. The roads of Bohemia and Moravia have a good, smooth surface, but there are no high-speed motorways or flyovers. All the trunk roads are signposted with standard European signs. But the further east you go the worse are the roads. In Slovakia the roads are narrow and bumpy in places; and there are no dual carriageways. Long stretches of road are so bad that they have been closed to traffic for resurfacing.

53

On Czechoslovak roads you can see cars, coaches, lorries, motor-bicycles and even pedestrians. But, in addition to the steady stream of modern motor traffic, these roads are also used by a great variety of slow-moving vehicles. There are horses or ponies in blinkers, pulling wagons loaded with fruit and vegetables; and there are cows yoked to hay-carts. Tractors (hitched to one or even two trailers) and huge combine-harvesters clutter the roads in the early morning and late evening. All this jumble of slow-moving traffic on the roads causes hold-ups and jams. No wonder Czechoslovak motorists feel that more and wider roads are needed in their country for the ever-growing numbers of cars and lorries.

Motor traffic through towns presents special problems in Bohemia and Moravia where there are many narrow streets and corners, and even narrower arched gateways at the entrances, left over from the Middle Ages. Some of the traffic jams have been eased by having "No Waiting" signs in the streets. Cars and lorries may then move slowly but they do keep moving. They stop and go at cross-roads and traffic lights and in the end they get through the town. Czech civil engineers feel that much more needs to be done to make the traffic move faster and to cope with the extra cars that come on to the roads every year. So they are drawing up plans for building ring roads and by-passes round the busiest of their industrial cities.

Czechoslovakia has few inland waterways. Her rivers are navigable for short stretches only, and they need constant

A summer afternoon on the Vltava River. In winter this river will become icebound and closed to traffic

dredging because of sand and silt in the water. The most important river is the Danube in the south. Large barges pulled by tugs travel from Slovak ports down the Danube as far as the Black Sea. Rivers such as the Vltava, Elbe, Oder, Morava and Vah are used by small self-propelled barges which carry timber, gravel and other bulky goods. These rivers are icebound in winter and closed to traffic. The ice, however, is not wasted. Lorries come to the river banks and gangs of men equipped with pickaxes hew blocks of ice out of the frozen rivers. The ice is loaded on to lorries and taken to underground concrete cellars where it can be stored and kept in perfect condition until the hot summer. It is then used by cafés and restaurants for cooling bottles of lemonade, beer or wine in tubs and buckets.

Each of Czechoslovakia's major cities has an airport and they are connected to each other by air routes. The State-

On a short flight. An air-taxi service operates in Czechoslovakia

owned airline company, C.S.A., uses Czechoslovak-made planes (called *Morava*) for most short-distance flights but flies modern British and Russian airliners on international routes.

Czechoslovakia's highly developed transport and industry and her abundant natural resources have helped to make her a great trading country. Goods- and passenger-trains cross her territory, going from one country to another and bringing in revenue from transit charges.

The Czechoslovak people have to sell goods abroad to live. They export manufactured goods, timber, cement, beer and foodstuffs to all their neighbours and to countries in the west. Most of Czechoslovakia's trade is with the U.S.S.R. but trade with African and Asian countries is increasing. Czechoslovak cars can be seen on the roads in all continents; and Czechoslovak shoes and glassware can be bought in shops in Britain and America.

At the same time, Czechoslovakia imports many goods from abroad, both raw materials for her industries and consumer goods for her population. Goods-trains, lorries and freighter-planes bring from abroad wheat, tobacco, hides, rubber, citrus fruits, bananas, coffee, cocoa, cotton and scores of other foodstuffs and raw materials needed by the country.

56

Prague and Other Czech Cities

Prague, the capital of Czechoslovakia, is today a modern city of over a million inhabitants. Just over a thousand years ago, in A.D. 965, an Arab merchant called Ibrahim Ibn Yakub went to Prague on business. He wrote that the city was a busy trading-centre in the lands of the Slavs and that he had met many merchants from distant countries there. He added that the houses were built of stone and looked solid.

People from all over the world still come in large numbers to see this beautiful city on the banks of the River Vltava. They come to visit Prague Castle, which stands proudly on the hillside, and the historic St Vitus cathedral. They come to see ancient churches and palaces, museums, theatres and concert-halls. Prague is a city of such great historical interest that it has been called the Rome of the North.

A view of Prague, the capital of Czechoslovakia. The city stretches on either side of the River Vltava

The Charles Bridge built by King Charles IV in the fourteenth century. In the background is the Royal Palace, with St Vitus Cathedral in the centre

The centre of Prague is a tangle of one-way streets, some broad, some narrow. Everywhere there are small cafés and restaurants with blue or red awnings. At the tables businessmen, tourists and ordinary citizens sit eating, drinking and talking. The food is good and beer and wine are very popular.

One of the most interesting sights of Prague is the Charles Bridge over the Vltava; it has two towers and thirty statues. Not far from the bridge is the famous Square of Good King Wenceslas. In the middle of the square is a statue of King Wenceslas. The square has often been in the news since the Russians invaded Czechoslovakia in 1968, for it was there that the inhabitants of Prague held meetings and demonstrations against the Russian invasion.

Prague is not only an historic city; she is growing rapidly in all directions. Every year new blocks of flats, shopping-centres and squares are built on the outskirts. Prague is at the junction of rail, road and river routes from north to south and from

58

east to west. She is an important link between the industrial cities of East Germany and southern Poland, the coal, iron and steel of Czechoslovakia and the farms and industries of the Danube valley in the south.

Prague is Czechoslovakia's leading industrial and commercial city. Her industries include engineering, printing, brewing and sugar-refining. There are also many textile mills, chemical and food-processing factories. Fine shoes and carpets, turbines and generators, jewellery and furniture made in Prague are famous not only in Czechoslovakia but also abroad.

West of Prague lies the ancient city of Pilsen, an important industrial and trading centre. The city was founded on the site of an old fortress built at the end of the thirteenth century; much of mediaeval Pilsen still exists. In the centre of Pilsen the tall spire of the cathedral of St Bartholomew looks down over a large square and busy city. All around are beautiful buildings decorated with stone carvings of flowers and animals. Many have graceful balconies and are fine examples of Renaissance and baroque architecture.

Near Pilsen there are rich coal and iron ore deposits which explain the presence of iron foundries and the local development of heavy engineering. The huge Skoda works, where heavy electrical machinery and electric engines are made, are also at Pilsen. But the great fame of Pilsen rests on the brewing of beer, which has been made here since the Middle Ages. Bottles and cans of Pilsen beer are exported all over the world.

North-west Bohemia is famous for its spa and its hot springs. The spa was established in 1348 on the orders of King Charles IV and was named after him Karlovy Vary—Charles' Spa. (It is also sometimes known by the German name of Karlsbad.)

Karlovy Vary stands in the narrow valley of the River Tepla. The houses are scattered on the hillside where there is little room for streets. Down in the valley there is a small square which is famous for its stone carvings showing how King Charles IV discovered the hot springs. Not far from the square is the baroque cathedral with its imposing dome.

There are twelve natural springs of hot water, rich in minerals, at Karlovy Vary. The best-known and biggest of the

Karlovy Vary (Karlsbad in German) is a famous spa which has twelve natural hot springs

springs is a geyser which hurls very hot water and steam to a great height. People suffering from diseases of the liver and other illnesses come to the spa to drink the water from the springs and to have hot baths. The patients stay in hotels and sanatoriums where they are looked after by doctors and nurses.

Brno is the capital of Moravia and Czechoslovakia's second largest city. She is situated in beautiful surroundings. The countryside north of the city is made up of limestone hills famous for their caves and grottoes. Tools and weapons of flint and stone belonging to prehistoric man have been found in these caves. Other interesting discoveries include a clay statue of a woman and a horse bone with drawings of bison on it. Eastwards lies the site of the battlefield of Austerlitz where Napoleon won one of his greatest battles against the combined armies of Austria and Russia.

On top of a hill stands Brno's most famous church, a Catholic cathedral with a slender, soaring spire. Another famous landmark is Spilberk Castle. Built in the thirteenth century, it was later to have a terrible dungeon with torture chambers added to it.

Brno also has a university and many colleges and schools. The centre of the city has wide streets with trams running down the middle, as well as smart shops and hotels.

Today Brno has a population of three hundred thousand inhabitants and is an important industrial and trading centre. She has rail, road and air communications with all parts of

Czechoslovakia. The many weaving- and spinning-mills in Brno have made people call her the Manchester of Moravia. Armaments, tractors, turbines, boilers and typewriters are all manufactured there too. Brno also boasts modern exhibition halls and grounds where international fairs are held each year.

Now let us visit Ostrava in Silesia, near the Polish border. This smoky city is surrounded by collieries. Its many iron and steel works date from the nineteenth century and form the basis of Czechoslovak heavy industry.

Ostrava has a population of two hundred and forty thousand, mostly of Czech, German and Polish descent. The town is expanding continually and new blocks of flats have recently been built. One of the largest chemical coking plants in Czechoslovakia is at Ostrava. There are also chemical factories, flour mills and breweries.

Bratislava and Other Slovak Towns

Many Slovak towns lie at cross-roads and on important trading-routes. They are famous for their castles which, in the past, protected the citizens from hordes of marauding barbarians or the cruel Turks. Let us pay a visit to a few of these towns.

Bratislava, the capital of Slovakia, is a large industrial city, the third largest in the whole of Czechoslovakia. It is the first busy river port on the banks of the Danube. Flat-bottomed

The River Danube is Czechoslovakia's most important inland water-way. These barges are on their way to Bratislava

barges with huge holds load and unload their cargoes of grain, timber, coal and other goods at the wharves along the river; passenger-steamers carrying tourists from Vienna and Budapest make regular calls there.

The history of Bratislava goes back a long way. People lived on this site in prehistoric times and archaeologists have found gold and silver coins there belonging to Celtic tribes. Because of its important position on the Danube, where several roads meet, the Romans occupied the settlement and built a strong fort to protect their camps and lands south of the Danube. Later, in the Dark Ages, Bratislava became an important trading-centre. In the ninth century, a big square castle was built on a small hill overlooking the river. It was rebuilt several times in the Middle Ages. Today, the castle and its

63

A Russian tank
in a Bratislava
street. This city
has a history of
invasion

four turrets still dominate the city and can be seen from as far away as Austrian territory across the River Danube.

Modern Bratislava is a mixture of broad and narrow streets, full of the rush and roar of trams and motor traffic. It has shady public gardens and attractive squares with fountains spraying cool water into the air. Many of its palaces were built in the seventeenth-century style which is called baroque. The famous St Martin's Cathedral was built in the Gothic style in the fifteenth century. In the modern part of the city there is a tomb surrounded by pillars, surmounted by a tall needle-shaped monument. On it stands the statue of a Russian soldier carrying a gun and a flag. Called Slavin, this lofty tomb was built after the Second World War in memory of the thousands of Russian soldiers who were killed while fighting to free Bratislava from the Germans.

The outskirts of Bratislava are untidy industrial areas with tall pylons, and cables going in all directions. There are many factories and mills for making machinery, textiles, shoes and foodstuffs. Wheat and barley are grown in the surrounding countryside to supply the city's bakeries and breweries.

North of Bratislava, where the country begins to get mountainous, is Trencin. This city is situated in beautiful surroundings on the banks of the River Vah. High above the city stands an ancient castle perched on bare rock. This castle bears a Roman inscription carved in the second century A.D. about a battle won by the Emperor Marcus Aurelius against the barbarians. Unfortunately, towards the end of the eighteenth century a great fire swept through the castle and the city, destroying ancient treasures and much property. In spite of the fire, however, the city was rebuilt and became prosperous again. Trencin has a large park, and many smart shops and cafés. On the banks of the River Vah there are shipyards where river-going craft are made.

Not far north of Trencin, tucked away among the green hills, is a spa called Trencianske Teplice. This spa has hot, sulphurous springs which are used for medicinal baths for people with rheumatism. There is a swimming-pool too, high up on the hillside, surrounded by pine trees. The swimming-pool is called the Green Frog and has been scooped out of the rock. The water comes from the hot springs and is warm all the year round. To reach the pool you climb up a steep, cobbled road. In winter, clouds of steam hang over the pool because of the cold air.

Continuing our journey northwards, following the River Vah valley, we meet on the road cumbersome, noisy lorries with huge bumpers. The valley becomes narrower and the mountains on either side become higher. There are women at work in the small fields; they wear white kerchiefs and black aprons. Then, rounding a bend, the valley suddenly widens and we see in the distance the industrial town of Zilina, with flat-topped blocks of flats on the outskirts, their balconies painted mustard yellow or emerald green.

Zilina is situated in north-western Slovakia and is an important railway and road junction, not far from the Polish border. It has a mixed population of Slovak and Polish descent. The city dates back to the Middle Ages. In 1310 it was proclaimed a free city by royal charter, and its Roman Catholic St Stephen's Church is famous for its wall-paintings in the Gothic style.

One of the largest timber-yards and furniture works in Slovakia is situated at Zilina. There are also engineering and chemical factories and breweries in the city, which is growing fast, with new houses rising and shops in broad streets.

From Zilina, the road runs eastwards along the valley. The Low Tatra Mountains ahead have steep slopes and tall peaks. Here the village houses are made of logs, and their pointed roofs are covered with flat overlapping bits of wood called shingles. In the autumn we pass cows pulling wagons of hay gathered in the steep, sloping fields. Goats, led by chains round their horns, are tethered by the roadside to crop the sweet

Wooden houses in a village in the Tatra region. Their roofs are covered with flat, overlapping pieces of wood called shingles

clover which grows thickly there. A little further on we come to the town of Mikulas which is an important tourist centre.

Mikulas was founded in the thirteenth century and its inhabitants have always traditionally worked in the textile and leather trades. Today the town has a railway and bus station and several hotels for tourists who come to visit the dripstone caves in a narrow valley just outside the town. This valley of limestone rocks is considered one of the most beautiful valleys in the whole of Czechoslovakia. The rocks have fantastic shapes, rising like castle towers above the valley.

Beneath the rocks there are caves with long underground passages, made by the stream Demanovka which runs under the mountain. The most famous of these is called the Ice Cave; it was first discovered in 1299. Thousands of tourists visit it every year, climbing a steep winding path up the mountain

Inside a limestone cave
near Mikulas. Stalac-
tites hang like icicles
and stalagmites rise
from the floor. They
are formed by dis-
solved limestone

to reach it. Here they can have a drink of ice-cold water, before following a guide through the barred door into the cave itself. Inside there are slippery steps which seem to go on and on into a strange world of ice and dripping icicles, dark grottoes and narrow passages. Whole stretches of ice glitter in the light of electric lamps fitted to the rock walls, but when the light is turned off there is complete darkness. There are also heaps of bear bones in the caves, telling us that bears once lived here. Entering the caves is like suddenly walking into the distant past.

East of Mikulas we come to the end of the Vah valley. Here the River Vah is only a mountain stream rushing over rocks and pebbles. Beyond is Poprad, the gateway to Eastern Slovakia. Poprad is a busy industrial town with engineering and chemical factories, breweries and cement works. It is served by a modern airport but it still has old, wide, tree-lined streets in the centre.

The main road leads out of the town on through country which is green and yellow in summer with ripening fields of wheat and barley, past little villages with white-washed cottages dozing in the hot sunshine. Everywhere there are ducks and geese—along the roadside, on ditches and banks, cropping the grass by streams. This road runs straight for long distances through gently rolling hills until finally, on top of one of these hills, we reach the ancient town of Levoca.

Levoca was founded as a stronghold in 1245, after the invasion of the Tartars. Its entrance is still guarded by the original massive tower with the narrow gateway below. In the centre of the town stands the ancient Town Hall flanked by the fourteenth-century St James's Church, with its tall green spire. There, too, is the massive round building of the Evangelical Church. The Town Hall has a museum where armour, old chests and wooden sculptures of saints are kept. Otherwise, Levoca is a quiet market town where fruit, vegetables and other agricultural products from the surrounding countryside are sold. It also has a few small factories for processing foodstuffs.

As we leave Levoca behind and continue our journey eastwards, we pass through hilly country thickly covered with forests of fir and spruce. The road is bumpy and bad in places. Cars and lorries drive slowly to avoid the potholes. The next town is the most important one in north-eastern Slovakia. It is Presov whose history goes back to the Middle Ages. Presov was made a free town by royal charter in 1374. Its prosperity was based on the trade route passing through, linking the Baltic countries in the north with the Balkans in the south.

Presov was badly damaged by bombing and shelling in the Second World War but all the ruined buildings have since been repaired. Today the town has a population of about forty thousand. One of the largest electrical engineering works in Slovakia is situated at Presov. There are also textile mills, furniture factories and brick works.

Now let us end our tour of Slovakia's towns by visiting Kosice, the largest town in the eastern region of the country.

Kosice is in the plains, not far from the Hungarian border. Roads and railways meet there and on the outskirts there are iron- and steel-works, modern housing estates, machine-tool and textile factories, flour- and sugar-mills, breweries and timber-yards.

But the centre of Kosice has not changed much over the centuries. There are churches in which candles burn while peasants in black, their faces as brown and wrinkled as crumpled brown paper, stand outside waiting. There is also the Roman Catholic Cathedral built in the fourteenth century in the Gothic style. Its roof is made of coloured tiles arranged in geometric patterns; its windows are of stained glass. On Sundays it is full of worshippers. Outside is the main square

Trams such as this one are used for public transport in Czechoslovak towns

with space for parked cars and a flower garden. Yellow and red trams clank up and down the main street. Cars are few and there are no traffic lights. The side-streets are swept by women with long brooms. The houses have barred windows hung with tattered curtains which seem as old as the churches and the paved road.

There are shops and cafés, too, in Kosice. And there are old hotels and a new skyscraper one, as well as a university and a broadcasting station. Beyond the town, there are meadows rich in maize, barley, sugar-beet, oats and great gaudy sunflowers bowing on long necks.

A Village in Slovakia

The village of Ilava lies in the plains of western Slovakia. In the distance, is the grey outline of the Carpathian Mountains. Ilava is on the main road which runs from Bratislava on the Danube to the mountains and the Polish border in the north.

This road follows the valley of the River Vah and is used by a great deal of motor traffic all the year round. It is a good road with open, unfenced country on either side. Old cherry and walnut trees line its sides, giving welcome shade from the hot summer sun. On the verges and in the ditches there are many wild flowers—meadowsweet and thistles mixed with blue cornflowers, all visited by dark brown bees. And everywhere, in summer, the shrill sound of the cricket can be heard.

The village itself is beside a stream which is crossed by a concrete bridge. The stream water is crystal clear. Women from the village wash their clothes in the stream where it is sandy and shallow. They slap the washing hard against wooden boards to get it clean.

The houses in the village have thick brick walls and double windows. The walls are plastered and painted yellow or green.

Beer-drinking is popular in village inns. The beer industry is highly mechanized, as shown by this picture taken in a large brewery

The roofs are covered with big heavy tiles. The houses are built like bungalows with a small porch in front where leafy grape vines grow up the pillars. Runner beans grow up the walls of the houses. Each house has a small flower garden in front and a vegetable garden and farmyard at the back.

In the middle of the village there is a grassy common with wooden benches where people sit and rest. Round the common are the public buildings—the town hall, the police station and the long, white-washed buildings of the school. At one end of the common there are two or three shops and the *Hostinica* or inn, which is always full of people drinking beer and eating fat sausages which taste of garlic. Children are allowed in and they drink beer too. While drinking and smoking, the men discuss the crops and the political situation in the country.

The villagers keep their houses spotlessly clean. A typical village house has three rooms and a shed at the back. The floor is covered with carpets and rush mats. The carved furniture is made of soft wood and is painted in white and brown. The sitting-room has wicker armchairs and two or three low glass-topped tables. A cabinet in the corner displays glasses, cups and plates with flower patterns. In another corner there is a dining-table which is used for meals on feast days.

The bedroom has two side beds which can be drawn out at night and made wider. Thick eiderdowns cover the beds. Parents and children normally share the same bedroom. The third room is the bedroom for guests. The kitchen is in the shed

These Czecho-slovak villagers, like all village folk, make time to chat to one another

at the back. There is no running water in the house. All water is fetched in buckets from a well in the garden.

Behind the house there are a few apricot trees and a large walnut tree. Beyond these is a vegetable garden. Pride of place here is taken by the bed of poppy plants which are grown for their seeds. The villagers use poppy seeds mixed with sugar and cream as a filling for buns and cakes. The vegetables include garlic, tomatoes, cucumbers and potatoes. There are many herbs, including the caraway plant; the long caraway seeds are used to flavour bread and soups. At the back of the garden there is a pigsty where a big sow and her piglets are kept. As meat has been scarce in the country for many years pigs fetch a lot of money at the livestock market.

Outside, on the common, flocks of geese crop the grass. A little girl watches over them, driving them back with a stick when they wander near the road.

74

Older children find that they can make money by selling fruit to passing lorry drivers and motorists. They put baskets of apricots, plums and apples by the roadside and wait for the customers to stop.

The village church is not far from the common. It is a Roman Catholic church, built of brick, plastered and painted yellow. The tall bell-tower rises above the front porch. The church has a slender spire and its roof is covered with sheets of zinc painted red. On top of the spire there is a brass cross. Every Sunday crowds of worshippers come to church and light candles at the various shrines.

Further up the unpaved road from the church stands a petrol station and garage called *Autoservice*. There is only one brand of petrol and diesel fuel there. The owner of the garage repairs cars, lorries and motor-bicycles. Sometimes he also mends tractors and farm machinery, like the row of combine harvesters now parked by the roadside.

Most of the villagers at Ilava work on co-operative farms, though they have small plots of land of their own which they plant with wheat and maize. Men and women wake at sunrise and go to work in the fields until three in the afternoon. Their life is hard but healthy. Some men drive tractors drawing long trailers loaded with bales of straw. Others drive horse-drawn wagons of manure. The horses are harnessed into high, pointed collars decorated with brass studs. The women hoe the maize fields and usually do lighter work. Slovak peasant children often work with their parents during the summer holidays, while their grandmothers mind the geese and cows and fetch the water.

An important office of the Slovak Ministry of Transport is situated at Ilava. A district surveyor lives there and so do several of his clerks. He employs about twenty villagers each year to repaint road signs and do road maintenance work; in winter, this means keeping the main road clear of snow and ice.

Tourists also hire the Ilava villagers as guides on excursions in the neighbourhood. A little north of the village, at the top of a small hill surrounded by poplar trees, there is a car-camping site. A rough road with potholes leads to the reception office. Motorists inquire there about accommodation and pay

Villagers selling geese in the market place. Geese can be the main source of income of a village. Their feathers are used to fill duvets

Children often help on the farm in the school holidays. These boys are driving hay rakes to the fields to turn the hay

for the hire of a tent or hut for the night. The site has a large parking-place for cars, a restaurant with a bar, and wash rooms. Many of the villagers from Ilava come to the site to sell eggs, milk, honey, fruit and vegetables and to work as cleaners and waiters in the restaurant.

Schools and Sport

Education has a long tradition in Czechoslovakia. The University of Prague was founded in 1348, and it gave to the world great scholars who spread knowledge in colleges and schools. During the Middle Ages, in Czechoslovakia as elsewhere, priests and monks in churches and monasteries taught poor children to read and write. By contrast, children from rich and noble families were taught to be gentlemen and warriors, not scholars; reading and writing were regarded as fit only for common people.

A great Moravian scholar, John Amos Comenius, changed many of these strange ideas about education. Comenius, who was born towards the end of the fifteenth century, lived for nearly eighty years. He was known to the Czechoslovaks as Komensky, and he wrote many books about the best ways to educate children. Comenius was a bishop whose influence was very great, particularly as he met many learned people of his day and passed his ideas on to them.

He was also the first man ever to write a picture-book for children. He believed in free and equal education for all children, both boys and girls, which in those days was unknown. Many of his teachings form the basis of modern Czechoslovak education, which is very democratic.

All Czechoslovak schools are run by the State. Schooling is free and compulsory for children between the ages of six and fifteen. It consists of a basic nine years at primary school, followed by three years at secondary or vocational school, depending on the child's ability. Traditional crafts, including the making of Bohemian glass and metal-work, are taught at vocational schools.

School starts on the first day of September and lasts until mid-June. There are Christmas and Easter holidays. During the three school terms, boys and girls all over Czechoslovakia

Charles University, Prague. The Czechoslovak flag can be seen on the right

get up early and, satchel in hand or on back, set out for school. They go by bus, tram or horse cart, by bicycle or on foot. In winter, many children arrive at school in sledges drawn by a horse with jingling bells.

Pupils completing their course at the secondary school can go on to university, provided they pass the entrance examination. There are nine universities in Czechoslovakia, the most famous being in Prague, Brno and Bratislava.

Pupils in all Czechoslovak schools have to learn about socialism and communism. Every pupil is expected to know the history of these movements and what they stand for. They are also expected to learn about the October Revolution in Russia and to love Russia as the "mother" of socialism and communism. But many teachers and pupils have been known

79

These boys and girls are enjoying outdoor pursuits at one of the many holiday camps for young people

to refuse to learn about communism and Russia. They cannot forget that their country was invaded and occupied by the Russians. In the winter of 1968, schools in some parts of Czechoslovakia actually had to close because of lack of fuel caused by the Russian invasion.

Czechoslovak schools use modern methods of learning. They are equipped with up-to-date laboratories for physics and chemistry, with tape-recorders and projectors for the teaching of modern languages and geography. Most schools have television sets and radios for school programmes which are broadcast in the official language of the two republics. Radio and

80

television studios are located in all the major towns of the Czech lands and Slovakia.

During their long summer holidays, many Czechoslovak boys and girls go to holiday-camps in forests and in the mountains. The camps have playing-fields where the children can play popular games, such as volleyball or handball. The camp commandant, who is usually a school games master, also organizes boating, swimming, mountain climbing and other out-of-door activities.

In winter, when it is usually cold and snowy, boys and girls go ice-skating, skiing and tobogganing. Bratislava has a winter

Czechoslovak children love tobogganing when the winter snows come

stadium with the largest ice-rink in the country. About twelve thousand spectators can be seated in it to watch the skating. Most of the big cities have open-air ice-rinks in winter, on the site of football pitches. These ice-rinks are occasionally used for speed-skating and figure-skating competitions. University students also train for ice-hockey matches there. Some of the world's best ice-hockey players are Czechoslovaks and their teams often compete against the Canadians and Russians for the top places in the European or world ice hockey championships.

Skiing is perhaps the most popular winter sport with both young and old. From Christmas until late in April thousands of people go to the Giant Mountains and the High and Low Tatras for skiing. They find there both nursery slopes for beginners and more difficult runways for good and experienced skiers. Cable-lifts, ski-lifts and funicular railways have been built to carry skiers up the slopes.

People often wonder why the Czechoslovaks are so good at gymnastics, and why they win so many prizes at international competitions. The reason is that in the middle of the nineteenth century gymnastics clubs were set up all over the Czech lands. Each club had a gymnasium equipped with vaulting-horses, parallel bars, wall bars and other sports apparatus. These clubs were called Sokols (which means "falcons") and their purpose was not only to develop the body but also to keep alive the love of freedom and independence. The Sokol movement was intensely patriotic. Many Czechs joined the Sokols and so

82

became good gymnasts. Though the Sokols were abolished by the Communists in 1948, young Czechoslovak men and women continue to train in gymnastics and give famous mass gymnastic displays in Prague and other cities.

Arts and Festivals

The Czechoslovak people are good-humoured and have a lively temperament. They have always liked entertainment. In the Middle Ages acrobats and jugglers would perform their antics outside inns and taverns, while travelling minstrels would play the lute and sing to the crowds in market squares. Drama festivals were held in the cities at Christmas and Easter, while carnivals and torchlight processions marked the days of popular saints, such as St Barbara and St Lucy.

Industrial development, the growth of cities and the rush of modern traffic have made it difficult or impossible to hold

The famous National Theatre, in Prague

A scene from *The Bartered Bride*, performed in the National Theatre

carnivals in city streets and squares as in the past. Today, people prefer to go to the theatre or cinema, or perhaps stay at home and watch television. But the modern music-halls and concert-halls in the cities of Czechoslovakia still have vast audiences, for the Czechoslovak people are fond of music and proud of their traditional folk tunes and composers. People say that the Czechs and Slovaks have music in their blood. The work of famous composers, such as Frederic Smetana and Anton Dvorak, seems to bear this out. Smetana's opera *The Bartered Bride* has been performed again and again all over the world. The Prague opera house has been called the Smetana Theatre in his honour. Dvorak's music is mainly based on the folk songs and dances of Bohemia; their natural rhythm and melody are very beautiful and easy to remember.

The Czech Philharmonic Orchestra of Prague is world-famous. Smaller philharmonic and symphonic orchestras are children to read and write. By contrast, children from rich and noble families were taught to be gentlemen and warriors, not scholars; reading and writing were regarded as fit only for common people.

A great Moravian scholar, John Amos Comenius, changed many of these strange ideas about education. Comenius, who was born towards the end of the fifteenth century, lived for nearly eighty years. He was known to the Czechoslovaks as Komensky, and he wrote many books about the best ways to educate children. Comenius was a bishop whose influence was very great, particularly as he met many learned people of his day and passed his ideas on to them.

He was also the first man ever to write a picture-book for children. He believed in free and equal education for all children, both boys and girls, which in those days was unknown. Many of his teachings form the basis of modern Czechoslovak education, which is very democratic.

All Czechoslovak schools are run by the State. Schooling is free and compulsory for children between the ages of six and fifteen. It consists of a basic nine years at primary school, followed by three years at secondary or vocational school, depending on the child's ability. Traditional crafts, including the making of Bohemian glass and metal-work, are taught at vocational schools.

School starts on the first day of September and lasts until mid-June. There are Christmas and Easter holidays. During the three school terms, boys and girls all over Czechoslovakia

Children often help on the farm in the school holidays. These boys are driving hay rakes to the fields to turn the hay

for the hire of a tent or hut for the night. The site has a large parking-place for cars, a restaurant with a bar, and wash rooms. Many of the villagers from Ilava come to the site to sell eggs, milk, honey, fruit and vegetables and to work as cleaners and waiters in the restaurant.

Schools and Sport

Education has a long tradition in Czechoslovakia. The University of Prague was founded in 1348, and it gave to the world great scholars who spread knowledge in colleges and schools. During the Middle Ages, in Czechoslovakia as elsewhere, priests and monks in churches and monasteries taught poor found in almost every Czechoslovak city. The orchestras perform not only in concert-halls but also in parks. Over twenty musical festivals are held in Czechoslovakia each year, the most important of which is the Prague Spring Festival in which artists from all over the world perform.

If we look at the way people in Czechoslovakia dress, we discover that they wear normal European summer and winter clothes, some hand-tailored, some made in factories. There are only a few people in Czechoslovak villages who still wear peasant dress—high boots, and shirts and coats of homespun rough cloth. National costumes have been gradually dying out, although they can still be admired in museums. But there are a few villages in southern Bohemia and in western Slovakia where countryfolk dress in colourful national costumes for weddings, christenings and feasts. The women wear a long red or black skirt with frills, a white silk blouse, a tight-fitting tunic and a bonnet with ribbons or embroidery. The men are more simply dressed. They wear tight-fitting white or blue trousers, a white shirt and a black coat. On their heads they wear a black hat with a wide, upturned brim.

Modern Czechoslovak craftsmen are well-organized in co-operatives. They make graceful glass ornaments and jugs decorated with intricate designs. Slovak artists at Modra, for example, are well known for their fine pottery. They also make small sculptured statues of porcelain (figurines) for which people pay large sums of money. Woodcarvers make picture frames, walking-sticks of all shapes and sizes, cuckoo-clocks, and toys and souvenirs for tourists which they send to the shops in spas and holiday resorts. The women and even quite young girls embroider hunting scenes on covers for cushions and bed-spreads. They also learn and pass on the traditional skills for making lace for veils, bridal gowns, blouses and tablecloths.

Czechoslovakia and the World

Czechoslovakia became a communist country in 1948. Since then the country has been ruled by the powerful communist government through its army and police. Under the communist system all public life is controlled by the State. Factories, mines, shops, banks and transport belong to the State and are run by civil servants. There is no freedom of speech. People appearing on radio and television are not allowed to discuss politics or criticize the government as they are in democratic countries.

All the papers and books published in Czechoslovakia praise the communist government and its policy. In addition, no criticism of Russia is allowed. When journalists and writers were courageous enough to criticize the communist system and government, they were arrested and put in prison for many years. Czechoslovakia's early communist rulers were so

A young Czechoslovak carries the national flag at the head of a demonstration demanding freedom from Russian oppression, August 1968

ruthless towards their people that they were called (in non-communist countries) "Stalinists" because, like Joseph Stalin, Russia's cruel dictator, they persecuted and imprisoned all their opponents.

In foreign policy the Czechoslovak communist rulers have always given their support to Russia. Their representatives have voted on many occasions *for* Russia's position and *against* Britain and the United States at the United Nations Organization and at the Geneva talks on disarmament. Czechoslovakia, like a number of other communist countries, became Russia's blind follower and so was called a satellite country by the western world.

The Czechoslovak Communists have never admitted that there is no freedom in their country. They insist that their system of government is democratic and that the people are

87

This Czechoslovak coal-miner is using a rapid drilling machine

free to think as they like. But, in the same breath, they will admit that if you wish to vote for a party opposed to the Communists, you are not allowed to do so.

After twenty years of communist rule, the people of Czechoslovakia—many of whom are well educated and highly skilled —felt that they should have a change of government. They realized that they could not have everything at once. So they advocated a combination of communist and free-enterprise methods of running factories and doing business. They merely pointed out that another communist country, Yugoslavia, had successfully tried out this mixed system. They also wanted to enjoy the freedom of speech and movement that they knew people in other countries have. In January 1968 a new leader of the Czechoslovak Communist Party was elected in Prague. His name was Alexander Dubcek. Under him, the new government promised to make life easier for the people, and to introduce reforms to give the people more freedom than they had ever had before under Communist rule. Suddenly, after twenty years of censorship, the Czechs and Slovaks found that they could talk freely and without fear of being put in prison; and that they could visit countries abroad when they wanted. Alexander Dubcek became first a very popular man and then a national hero.

The Russian leaders were worried when they heard about the reforms being introduced in Czechoslovakia. They, and the leaders of East Germany and Poland, feared that the spirit of reform and freedom might spread to their own countries. They saw in these new ideas a threat to their own rule. They decided that they could not allow the restoration of parliamentary democracy and free enterprise in Czechoslovakia.

The Russian leaders and their friends from East Germany, Poland, Hungary and Bulgaria met in Warsaw and from there sent an ultimatum to the Czechoslovak rulers to put an end to their reforms. The Russians, determined to have their own way, held talks with the Czechoslovak leaders in a small town on the Czechoslovak-Russian border and later in Bratislava. But the people of Czechoslovakia were too happy with their newly-won freedom and refused to obey the Russians.

Then, in the early hours of August 21st, 1968, Czechoslovakia was invaded by Russian troops and tanks, supported by armed units from East Germany, Poland, Hungary and Bulgaria. Nearly one hundred Czech and Slovak people were killed during the invasion and many more were wounded in the

Citizens of Prague talk to the invading Russians, August 1968

demonstrations against the invaders. The Czechoslovak army was ordered not to fight. Some observers now say that the decision not to fight was a mistake. Had the Czechoslovak army fought for every inch of ground the Russians might have withdrawn their troops.

The whole world, including the Communists themselves, was shocked by the Russian-led invasion. The United States President, Lyndon Johnson, condemned the invasion as a violation of human rights and of the United Nations Charter.

Alexander Dubcek and other liberal Czechoslovak leaders were arrested and taken, in handcuffs, to Moscow where they were forced to sign an agreement with Russia allowing Russian troops to stay in Czechoslovakia and putting an end to all freedom and reforms.

Alexander Dubcek was allowed to return to Prague while the country remained under Russian occupation. He was wisely allowed some freedom. But the Czechoslovak people were sad. They had lost their self-respect. How could they say what they felt? A young Czech student, Jan Pallach, decided that it was better to die than to live under the Russians. On a cold day in January 1969 he went to King Wenceslas Square in the heart of Prague, soaked himself in petrol and set it alight. People who saw him burn tried to put out the flames and rushed him to hospital. A few days later Jan Pallach was dead. The people called him a national martyr.

The Czechoslovak people have since shown their deep hatred of the Russians and made them angry. In March 1969 the Czechoslovak ice-hockey team defeated the Russian team at the Stockholm ice-hockey championships, with the score of four to three. Czechs and Slovaks all over the country watched on television the victory of their team. They went wild with joy. Crowds in Prague chanted and carried banners with the

Crowds gather in Wenceslas Square, Prague, to pay tribute to those Czechoslovaks who died during the Russian invasion

symbolic figures four to three. Soon the crowds got out of control. Angry young men tore down Russian flags and sacked Russian shops and travel agencies.

The Russian leaders were furious when they heard of this behaviour. They decided to have Alexander Dubcek dismissed as leader of the Czechoslovak Communist Party and replace him with Dr Gustav Husak, one of their trusted friends. Strict censorship of radio, television, newspapers and books was again introduced and all Czechs and Slovaks who had criticized the Russians in public were thrown out of their jobs or put into prison.

Today, the Czechoslovak people enjoy a higher standard of living than their Eastern neighbours. Their factories produce many goods. Food which was once scarce is now plentiful. But they feel enclosed in their own country. It may seem strange to us that a small country like Czechoslovakia, in the heart of Europe, should not allow its citizens to lead a free life and enjoy all human rights. We can only hope that one day the Russians will allow the Czechs and Slovaks more freedom and let them go their own way.

Index

93

nationalization 30, 86–7
nuclear power 41

oats 48
Oder River 9, 22, 55
oil 21, 22, 41
Orava Castle 12
Ore Mountains 20
Ostrava 62

Pallach, Jan 91
parliament 33–4
pigs 21, 47, 50, 74
Pilsen 39, 59
polecat 18
poppy crop 48, 74
Poprad 68
potatoes 21, 48, 74
Prague 33, 38, 39, 57–9
Presov 70

quartz 20

Rachell, Mt 20
railways 14, 53
religion 24, 27; *see also* churches
Remek, Vladimir 36
rivers 9, 14, 19, 40, 54–5
rock salt 22, 38
Roman invaders 48, 63, 65
Russia 12, 14, 41, 79–80, 87, 89–92
Ruthenia 14
rye 21, 48

St Vitus Cathedral 26
Samo (Czechoslovak chieftain) 23
schools *see* education
Second World War 11, 14, 29, 39, 64
sheep 15, 47; wild 17
shingle roofs 66
Silesia 22–3, 38, 62
silver 16, 37
skiing 20, 82
Skoda car 42; engineering 59

Slavin tomb 64
Slovakia 11, 14–15, 32–4, 48–9, 62–77
Smetana, Frederic 84
socialism 79
Sokols 82–3
spas 60, 65
Spilberk Castle 61
sport 81–3, 91
"Stalinists" 87
Subcarpathian Ruthenia 14
sugar beet 48, 50, 71

Tatra car 42
Tatra Mountains 16–18, 66
theatre 84
timber industry 42–6
trade 12, 41, 48, 56
transport 14, 42, 53–6
Trencianske Teplice 65
Trencin 65

United Nations Organization 31
universities 26, 77
uranium 37
U.S.S.R. *see* Russia

Vah River 40, 55, 65
vegetables 12, 19, 23, 74
Versailles, Treaty of 28
vines 21, 48
Vltava River 19, 40, 55

Warsaw Pact 31, 89–90
Wenceslas, King 24–5, 58
wheat 21, 47, 50–1, 56
White Carpathians 15
wild animals 17–18, 20, 22
wine 48
wolf 18

Zatopek, Emil 35
zinc 22, 37
Zilina 66

J
914.37
P

45729

Popescu, Julian

Let's visit Czechoslovakia

Hiram Halle Memorial Library
Pound Ridge, New York